WORKBOOK
Genesis Curriculum
The Book of Genesis

Junior Edition

This workbook belongs to

_____

Day 1

Spelling Words

_____   _____

_____   _____

Change each sentence to begin with a capital letter and to end with the correct punctuation mark.

1. friday is the best day of the week

2. i am so excited

3. why do rainbows come after a rainfall

4. come here, now

5. can I please have a drink

6. i don't like spicy food

7. where are my shoes

8. do sea turtles live in seas

9. you can do it   (cheering someone on)

10. gifts are fun to give

11. rabbits live in dens

Day 2

Spelling Words

_____   _____

_____   _____

Find the Verbs
Circle the verbs. Actions are verbs, the things people do.

1. The little black kitten plays with a ball. *Example*

2. I write stories.

3. The old brown couch squeaks.

4. Can you read me this book?

Which continents are shown here?

Africa
Antarctica
Asia
Australia
Europe
North America
South America

Day 3

Spelling Words

_____   _____

_____   _____

Which continent is shown here?

Africa
Antarctica
Asia
Australia
Europe
North America
South America

Write a sentence. Make sure it begins with a capital letter and ends with a punctuation mark. If you don't know what to write, write about what type of seed you would like to plant. Why? What would you like to grow?

_____

_____

If you used an action verb in your sentence, circle it.

Day 4

Spelling Words

_____   _____

_____   _____

Which continent is shown here?

Africa
Antarctica
Asia
Australia
Europe
North America
South America

Light, heaven, sign, and season are all things. They are all nouns. Which of these are things, nouns? Which are actions, verbs? Underline the nouns and circle the verbs. Or, you could mark them with two separate colors. They are all either actions or things.

paper   give   money   dogs   scissors

truck   feel   sleeps   ran   honey

Day 5

Spelling Words

_____   _____

_____   _____

_____   _____

_____   _____

_____   _____

_____   _____

Write in the letter of the definition for each word.

_____ surface   A. to make, to cause to come into existence

_____ separate   B. to rule, to be in control over a group

_____ produce   C. the outer layer of something

_____ govern   D. to move things apart

Day 6

Spelling Words

_____   _____

_____   _____

Draw a line to separate the subject from the predicate. The subject is who or what the sentence is about. The predicate tells us about the subject..

Example: Sarah / is playing in the yard.
          subject   predicate

My dog is so funny.

This book is so exciting.

She has two brothers and one sister.

Jonathan pitches the fastest on the team.

The girl named Deborah is the best at balancing.

Draw a picture of a fish. Make sure to include fins and scales.

Day 7

Spelling Words

_____   _____

_____   _____

Find the Nouns that are things.
Circle the things. Things are nouns.

1. The little black kitten plays with a ball. *Example*

2. There are stories on these papers.

3. The old brown couch squeaks.

4. Does this dog have a collar?

Draw an insect. Remember it must have three body parts, six legs, and two antennae.

Day 8

Spelling Words

_____   _____

_____   _____

Color the words with similar meanings the same color.

bright   cold   light   hot

warm   kind   icy   nice

Draw an arachnid.

Day 9

Spelling Words

_____   _____

_____   _____

Circle the mammals.

Day 10

Spelling Words

_____   _____

_____   _____

_____   _____

_____   _____

_____   _____

_____   _____

_____   _____

Write in the letter of the definition for each word.

_____ multiply   A. to move slowly and carefully to not be noticed

_____ creep   B. to increase a lot, to become more and more

_____ synonym   C. word of similar meaning

_____ subdue   D. to bring under control

Day 11

Spelling Words

_____   _____

_____   _____

Correct the sentences. What's missing?

is this your book?

I'm so excited

Super awesome.

That great, big, enormous dog over there.

Draw a diagram of the water cycle.

Day 12

Spelling Words

_____   _____

_____   _____

Write a sentence about where you have traveled. Here's an example.
I traveled north to visit my grandmother.

_____

_____

Draw a compass rose. If you like to draw, draw an upside-down map and draw the compass rose to show which way is north. Your compass rose only needs to have north on it, but it would be good to write on it N, S, E, W for north, south, east, and west.

Day 13

Spelling Words

_____   _____

_____   _____

Fill in the blanks to write the word heart.

H ____   ____   ____ T

Draw a map of your neighborhood.

Key

Day 14

Spelling Words

_____   _____

_____   _____

Write two commands. Make sure they start with a capital letter because they are sentences. Be sure to end them with an exclamation mark because you mean it!

_____

_____

Extra space: Draw a picture showing your vocabulary word or write your full name.

Day 15

Spelling Words

_____   _____

_____   _____

_____   _____

_____   _____

_____   _____

_____   _____

_____   _____

Write in the letter of the definition for each word.

_____ mist   A. to move smoothly and continuously

_____ form   B. a cloud of tiny water droplets near the earth's surface

_____ flow   C. to give an order

_____ command   D. to create something, to put things together into a shape

Day 16

Spelling Words

_____   _____

_____   _____

Underline the nouns that are places and things.

1. We are going to have dinner at Pizza Hut.

2. Let's go for a picnic at the park.

3. We need to go to the store.

4. I'll see you at church.

5. Put the stinky bag in the trash can in the garage.

Day 17

Spelling Words

_____   _____

_____   _____

Draw a picture of a serp___ ___ ___. Sound it out and fill in the letters of your vocabulary word.

Draw a picture of a river running to the sea.

Day 18

Spelling Words

_____   _____

_____   _____

Write a question. Make sure it starts with a capital letter and ends with a question mark. What do you want to ask?

_____

_____

Draw a venomous snake.

Day 19

Spelling Words

_____   _____

_____   _____

Put the dates in order from oldest to most recent. Write them in order on the lines. Write the oldest BC or AD date at the top of each column.

3000 BC   1 BC   100 BC   100 AD   2000 AD   1 AD

_____   _____

_____   _____

_____   _____

Draw an animal in its habitat.

Day 20

Spelling Words

_____   _____

_____   _____

_____   _____

_____   _____

_____   _____

_____   _____

_____   _____

Write in the letter of the definition for each word.

_____ station   A. feeling very embarrassed and guilty

_____ serpent   B. snake

_____ deceive   C. to place someone in a particular place

_____ ashamed   D. make someone believe something untrue

Day 21

Spelling Words

_____   _____

_____   _____

Underline the nouns that are people and things.

1. Ned is having fun.

2. Give the paper to Lily.

3. Obed and Johanna are playing a game.

4. Help your brother with his work.

5. Girls, take out the trash.

Circle the peninsula.

Day 22

Spelling Words

_____   _____

_____   _____

Write a "said" sentence. Here are examples.

He said that it was okay. I said they could play too.

_____

_____

Circle the pennisula.

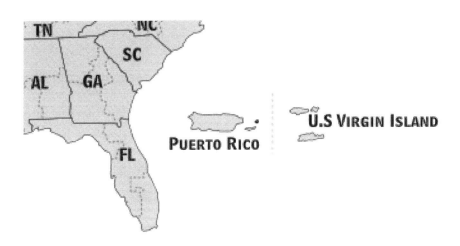

24

Day 23

Spelling Words

_____   _____

_____   _____

Write two and then the word given with an S on the end.

Example:

one book   two books

one kid   _____

one toy   _____

one door   _____

one carrot   _____

one bed   _____

Day 24

Spelling Words

_____   _____

_____   _____

Write two and then the word given with an S on the end.

Example:

one book   two books

one tool   _____

one time   _____

Design and draw a tool. What would help you out? What tool do you wish you had?

Day 25

Spelling Words

_____   _____

_____   _____

_____   _____

_____   _____

_____   _____

_____   _____

_____   _____

Write in the letter of the definition for each word.

_____ wanderer   A. revenge

_____ strike   B. to hit suddenly with a lot of strength

_____ vengeance   C. being there, whether seen or not

_____ presence   D. someone who wanders

Day 26

Write a sentence using one of the vocabulary words. Draw a picture that illustrates the meaning of the other. surface – separate

_____

_____

Which continent is shown here?

Africa
Antarctica
Asia
Australia
Europe
North America
South America

Day 27

Write a sentence using one of the vocabulary words. Draw a picture that illustrates the meaning of the other. govern – produce

_____

_____

Draw a picture or act out a plant germinating and decomposing. Germination is the early growth of a seed plant, when it's just poking out of its shell, sprouting roots and a stem. Decomposition is when a plant dies and starts to fall apart slowly.

Day 28

Write a sentence using one of the vocabulary words. Draw a picture that illustrates the meaning of the other. creep – multiply

_____

_____

Circle all the nouns. Nouns can be people, places, or things.

Antarctica   mammal   spits

teases   habitat   compass   blue

Write the dates in order from oldest to most recent.

1 AD   1 BC   100 AD   100 BC

_____   _____   _____   _____

Day 29

Write a sentence using one of the vocabulary words. Draw a picture that illustrates the meaning of the other. synonym – subdue

_____

_____

Write the plural of these words.

Example:

one book   two books

one friend   _____

one chair   _____

Divide this globe into hemispheres. Draw a line around the middle to divide it into northern and southern hemispheres. Each hemisphere is half of the earth.

Day 30

Write a sentence using one of the vocabulary words. Draw a picture that illustrates the meaning of the other. mist – form

_____

_____

Circle all the nouns. Nouns can be people, places, or things.

sweet   mother   officer   serpent

Africa   seeds   decompose   heart

Which of these animals are vertebrates? A vertebrate has a backbone. Birds, mammals, fish, and reptiles have a backbone. Insects and arachnids do not.

Day 31

Write a sentence using one of the vocabulary words. Draw a picture that illustrates the meaning of the other. flow – command

_____

_____

Which continent is shown here?

Africa
Antarctica
Asia
Australia
Europe
North America
South America

Review how light is moving energy and that energy is the ability to do work. Energy heats things up. Run around and feel the warmth of lots of energy!

Day 32

Write a sentence using one of the vocabulary words. Draw a picture that illustrates the meaning of the other. ashamed – serpent

_____

_____

Circle all the nouns. Nouns can be people, places, or things.

light   sky   govern   great

Cain   brother   farm   sticky

What is carried around in your circulatory system?

What are your lungs and diaphragm used for?

Day 33

Write a sentence using one of the vocabulary words. Draw a picture that illustrates the meaning of the other. deceive – to station

_____

_____

Write the plural of these words.

Example:

one book   two books

one key   _____

one lion   _____

What makes an area a desert?

What is a myth?

Day 34

Write a sentence using one of the vocabulary words. Draw a picture that illustrates the meaning of the other. wanderer – vengeance

_____

_____

Where would you find the largest tundra in the southern hemisphere?

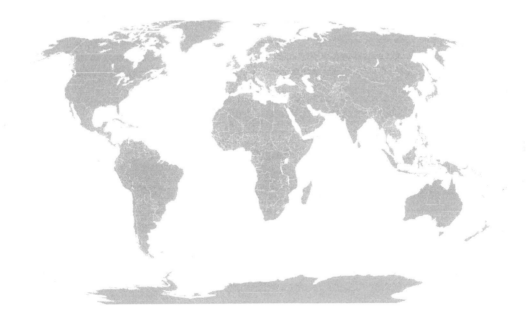

Day 35

Write a sentence using one of the vocabulary words. Draw a picture that illustrates the meaning of the other. presence – strike

_____

_____

Draw a picture of the water cycle. Use up arrows to show evaporation. Where does evaporating water come from? How does it return to the ground?

Day 36

Spelling Words

_____   _____

_____   _____

Write a sentence that's a question. It should end with a ? question mark.

Where did everybody go?

_____

_____

Circle the body parts that are controlled by muscles.

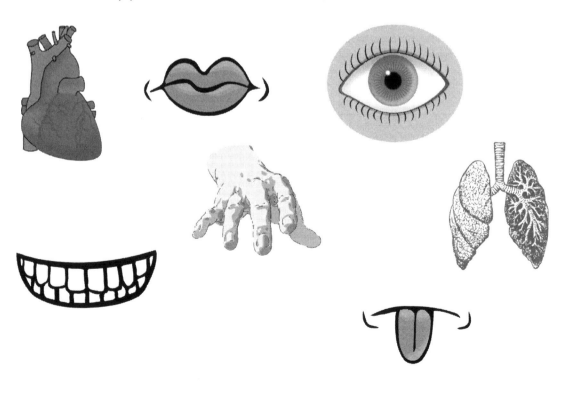

Day 37

Spelling Words

_____   _____

_____   _____

Write one word to describe the nouns.

Example:

heavy

_____

_____

Day 38

Spelling Words

_____   _____

_____   _____

Fill in the letters to complete the words.

Example:

book   bo____

clou____   ha____d

Draw a picture that shows low population density. What does that mean?

Day 39

Spelling Words

_____   _____

_____   _____

Fill in the letter E to change the word. Read both words.

Example:

bit   bit<u>e</u>

hop   hop____

tap   tap____

hid   hid____

Draw a boat design.

Day 40

Spelling Words

_____   _____

_____   _____

_____   _____

_____   _____

_____   _____

_____   _____

_____   _____

Write in the letter of the definition for each word.

_____ righteous   A. fame

_____ establish   B. doing something wrong to get what you want

_____ renown   C. to create something intended to last

_____ corrupt   D. doing what is right

Day 41

Spelling Words

_____   _____

_____   _____

Write names. All names begin with a capital letter. List people you know.
You have eight blanks.

_____

_____

_____

_____

_____

_____

_____

_____

Day 42

Spelling Words

_____   _____

_____   _____

Write the word without the silent E. Read both words.

Example:

bite   bit

cane   _____

rode   _____

here   _____

Draw a picture of groundwater.

Day 43

Spelling Words

_____   _____

_____   _____

Draw a picture of water in the three states of matter.

solid   liquid   gas

Draw a picture of water as molecules in the three states of matter. Use dots for the water molecules. They are tightly packed in a solid so they can only move a little bit. They are really spread out in a gas so that they can move a lot.

solid   liquid   gas

Day 44

Spelling Words

_____   _____

_____   _____

Write a sentence. A sentence has a noun and a verb. It has a subject and then tells us about what the subject is or what the subject is doing.

_____

_____

Draw a rainbow. ROY G. BIV

Day 45

Spelling Words

_____   _____

_____   _____

_____   _____

_____   _____

_____   _____

_____   _____

_____   _____

Write in the letter of the definition for each word.

_____ remove   A. to take away, to get rid of

_____ descendants   B. to become less or to make something become less

_____ require   C. to need, to say that something has to be done

_____ decrease   D. all the generations that are born from you

Day 46

Spelling Words

_____   _____

_____   _____

Write in the apostrophe and the last letter of the second word to complete the contraction.

Example:

let us   let's

I am   I_____

do not   don_____   This one uses the N from not.

he is   he_____

Try these all on your own. Write the first word, the apostrophe, and the last letter from the second word.

she had   _____

it is   _____

Day 47

Spelling Words

_____   _____

_____   _____

Abraham's Travels

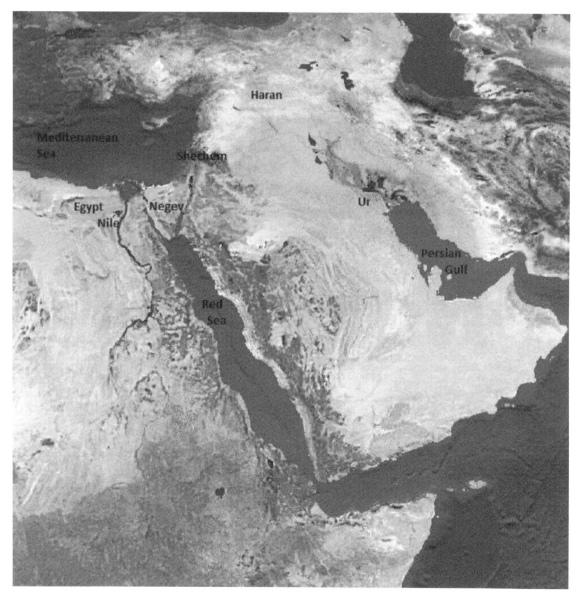

Day 48

Spelling Words

_____   _____

_____   _____

Write in the S to make the words plural that have a vowel before the Y. Here are the vowels: A E I O U. If there isn't a vowel there, don't do anything.

Example:

donkeys_   baby_____ (left alone)

key_____

day_____

sky_____

toy_____

way_____

try_____

Day 49

Spelling Words

_____   _____

_____   _____

Draw a picture of a sustainable practice.

Draw a picture of an unsustainable practice.

Day 50

Spelling Words

_____   _____

_____   _____

_____   _____

_____   _____

_____   _____

_____   _____

_____   _____

Write in the letter of the definition for each word.

_____ sustain   A. intense, extreme

_____ babble   B. support physically or mentally

_____ severe   C. to get more and more

_____ accumulate   D. to talk nonstop

Day 51

Spelling Words

_____   _____

_____   _____

You've learned that all names begin with a capital letter. Abram and God Most High are two of the names from our reading today. There are other types of names, though. There are names of places. List names of places today. Some examples would be your street name, your city name, and your state name. Some other examples of places are Disney World and the Grand Canyon. There are six lines. Make sure each place name begins with a capital letter.

_____

_____

_____

_____

_____

_____

Day 52

Spelling Words

_____   _____

_____   _____

Add EE to the letters below to write words. Read your words!

tr   b   fr   kn   s__d   sw__t

_____   _____

_____   _____

_____   _____

Draw a picture of a river. Label the headwaters, delta, and tributary.

Day 53

Spelling Words

_____   _____

_____   _____

Fill in the blanks to write sentences.

When God made me, He made someone

_____.

When God made my _____, He made

someone special.

When God _____ my _____,

He made someone _____ .

Thank you, God, for _____

_____ .

Day 54

Spelling Words

_____   _____

_____   _____

I live in

_____ ,

_____ .

Draw a picture of your state.

Day 55

Spelling Words

_____   _____

_____   _____

_____   _____

_____   _____

_____   _____

_____   _____

_____   _____

Write in the letter of the definition for each word.

_____ deliver   A. the person or organization in power

_____ heir   B. to rescue, save

_____ prevent   C. to keep something from happening

_____ authority   D. the person who will inherit

Day 56

Spelling Words

_____   _____

_____   _____

Come up with two nouns and two verbs. A noun is a person, place, or thing. A verb can be an action, something you do. Then put them into sentences. It's okay if they are silly. Here's an example.

Noun: ball   Verb: sing   The ball sings.

Noun: Verb:

_____   _____

Sentence:

_____

Noun: Verb:

_____   _____

Sentence:

_____

Day 57

Spelling Words

_____   _____

_____   _____

What is the opposite? There doesn't always have to be one correct answer.

Example: Day   <u>Night</u>

hard   _____

high   _____

boring   _____

hungry   _____

loud   _____

Day 58

Spelling Words

_____   _____

_____   _____

Come up with two nouns and two verbs. A noun is a person, place, or thing. A verb can be an action, something you do. Then put them into one sentence. Here's an example.

Nouns: cat, dog   Verbs: sing, dance   The cat sings and the dog dances.

Noun: Verb:

_____   _____

Noun: Verb:

_____   _____

Sentence:

_____

_____

Day 59

Spelling Words

_____   _____

_____   _____

Write a thank you note to God.

Dear Lord,

Thank you that by your grace I...

_____

_____

_____

_____

Day 60

Spelling Words

_____   _____

_____   _____

_____   _____

_____   _____

_____   _____

_____   _____

_____   _____

Write in the letter of the definition for each word.

_____ intercept   A. having a position on the other side

_____ opposite   B. to go back to where you came from

_____ deny   C. blocking something from going

_____ return   D. refuse

Day 61

Write a sentence using one of the vocabulary words. Draw a picture that illustrates the meaning of the other. renown – corrupt

_____

_____

Draw a picture of a body part that is controlled by a muscle.

Day 62

Write a sentence using one of the vocabulary words. Draw a picture that illustrates the meaning of the other. establish – righteous

_____

_____

Write one adjective to describe each noun. An adjective describes.

_____

_____

Day 63

Write a sentence using one of the vocabulary words. Draw a picture that illustrates the meaning of the other. decrease – remove

_____

_____

Draw a picture of water in the three states of matter.

solid   liquid   gas

Day 64

Write a sentence using one of the vocabulary words. Draw a picture that illustrates the meaning of the other. descendants – require

_____

_____

Write the plural of these words.

Example:

one book   two books

one door   _____

one dog   _____

Day 65

Write a sentence using one of the vocabulary words. Draw a picture that illustrates the meaning of the other. babble – accumulate

_____

_____

Circle all the nouns. Nouns can be people, places, or things.

mighty   sons   animals   eyes

them   rooms   people   every

Day 66

Write a sentence using one of the vocabulary words. Draw a picture that illustrates the meaning of the other. sustain – severe

_____

_____

Draw a rainbow. ROY G. BIV

Day 67

Write a sentence using one of the vocabulary words. Draw a picture that illustrates the meaning of the other. deliver – heir

_____

_____

Write in the apostrophe and the last letter of the second word to complete the contraction.

Example:

let us   let's

do not   don_____ This one uses the N from not.

Try these all on your own. Write the first word, the apostrophe, and the last letter from the second word.

he had   _____

she is   _____

Day 68

Write a sentence using one of the vocabulary words. Draw a picture that illustrates the meaning of the other. prevent – authority

_____

_____

Draw a picture of a river. Label the headwaters, delta, and tributary.

Day 69

Write a sentence using one of the vocabulary words. Draw a picture that illustrates the meaning of the other. intercept – opposite

_____

_____

Write in the S to make the words plural that have a vowel before the Y. Here are the vowels: A E I O U. If there isn't a vowel there, don't do anything.

Example:

donkeys_   baby_____ (left alone)

play_____

boy_____

cry_____

Day 70

Write a sentence using one of the vocabulary words. Draw a picture that illustrates the meaning of the other. return – deny

_____

_____

Design a building. How will you make it strong and long-lasting?

Day 71

Spelling Words

_____   _____

_____   _____

Add OW to each word and circle the words with an O sound.

Example: t OW n   (k n OW)

p_____er   fl_____   wind_____

l_____   c_____   n_____

m_____   h_____   w_____

Day 72

Spelling Words

_____   _____

_____   _____

Design and draw pillars and maybe a person and place to go along with your "thing." The things you draw are nouns.

Day 73

Spelling Words

_____   _____

_____   _____

Write a list of names of people or places that you want to pray for. The names of people, places, and things are proper nouns.

_____

_____

_____

_____

_____

_____

Day 74

Spelling Words

_____   _____

_____   _____

Write the question you asked your parent.

_____

_____

Write the answer you were given.

_____

_____

Day 75

Spelling Words

_____   _____

_____   _____

_____   _____

_____   _____

_____   _____

_____   _____

_____   _____

Write in the letter of the definition for each word.

_____ inhabitant   A. a metal stove used for burning

_____ furnace   B. to stay in one place

_____ pillar   C. someone who lives in a place

_____ settle   D. a tall, relatively thin structure

Day 76

Spelling Words

_____   _____

_____   _____

Write, "The earth orbits the sun." Draw the earth's orbit around the sun.

_____

Day 77

Spelling Words

_____   _____

_____   _____

Draw an ox at work. Write a sentence about what the ox is doing in your drawing.

_____

_____

Day 78

Spelling Words

_____   _____

_____   _____

Write a knock knock joke. Here's an example. Make sure you use the correct punctuation.

Knock, knock.
Who's there?
Lettuce.
Lettuce who?
Lettuce in! It's cold out here!

_____

_____

_____

_____

_____

Day 79

Spelling Words

_____   _____

_____   _____

Draw pictures or act to show the words as nouns and as verbs.

NOUN   **VERB**

FLY

RACE

TIE

Day 80

Spelling Words

_____   _____

_____   _____

_____   _____

_____   _____

_____   _____

_____   _____

_____   _____

Write in the letter of the definition for each word.

_____ integrity   A. to bring something back to its normal condition

_____ restore   B. to cause extreme sorrow or worry

_____ wean   C. the character quality of holding to strong principles

_____ distress   D. to gradually get used to not having something

Day 81

Spelling Words

_____   _____

_____   _____

Sometimes to add on an ending we need to add a double letter first. You added a silent E onto words to change them, like tap becomes tape. To write tap in the past tense, you write tapped. You add an extra P. If you just wrote taped, then you put a piece of tape on something instead of tapping it. The same thing applies if you wrote tapping vs. taping.

Add a double letter and then the ending. Read the word!

Example:

hop   -ing   hopping

hug   -ing   _____

tip   -ed   _____

beg   -er   _____

grab   -ed   _____

plan   -ing   _____

Day 82

Spelling Words

_____   _____

_____   _____

Write the two words as a contraction or the contraction as two words.

Example:

hadn't   had not

cannot   _____

it's   _____

wouldn't   _____

is not   _____

they'll   _____

Day 83

Spelling Words

_____   _____

_____   _____

A pronoun replaces a noun. Write a pronoun to replace the nouns given. (Note: I'm looking for subject pronouns. If they say the object pronoun, eg. her, put it in a sentence, Rachel helps, <u>She</u> helps.)

Example:

your name   I

you and your family   _____

Daniel and Jacob   _____

Rachel   _____

book   _____

Timothy   _____

Day 84

Spelling Words

_____   _____

_____   _____

You are going to write the past tense of the verbs. Think: Today I ____.
Yesterday I _____.

Example:

run   ran

walk   _____

eat   _____

sing   _____

play   _____

trip (double the p)   _____

Day 85

Spelling Words

_____   _____

_____   _____

_____   _____

_____   _____

_____   _____

_____   _____

_____   _____

Write in the letter of the definition for each word.

_____ redeem   A. a gift, something offered

_____ seize   B. to grab suddenly and forcefully

_____ offering   C. a trip taking you from one place to another

_____ journey   D. to get or get back something in exchange for payment

Day 86

Spelling Words

_____   _____

_____   _____

Write in the correct "2."

Examples:
    I'm going <u>to</u> ride my bike. I'm going <u>to</u> their house.
    Let me try <u>too</u>!
    I have <u>two</u> dogs.

I want another slice _____!

I like _____ dance.

I am going _____ get something _____ eat.

Here are _____ pieces for you.

I have _____ goldfish.

This is _____ slippery to walk on.

I am on my way _____ bed.

Day 87

Spelling Words

_____   _____

_____   _____

List jobs that you think you would like to do on the left and jobs you think you would not like to do on the right. They can be anything. You don't have to fill all the lines, but I wanted to leave room for you to dream and pretend.

_____   _____

_____   _____

_____   _____

_____   _____

_____   _____

_____   _____

_____   _____

Day 88

Spelling Words

_____   _____

_____   _____

Copy the sentence starter and finish the sentence. Then draw an outline of the country.

I would like to travel to _____ because ...

_____

_____

_____

Day 89

Spelling Words

_____   _____

_____   _____

Write the plurals by following the rules. Take off the end of the word to change the F into VES.

Example:

wife   wives

leaf   _____

half   _____

loaf   _____

thief   _____

yourself   _____

Day 90

Spelling Words

_____   _____

_____   _____

_____   _____

_____   _____

_____   _____

_____   _____

_____   _____

Write in the letter of the definition for each word.

_____ bound   A. to state clearly, to make known publicly

_____ thicket   B. to tie together tightly

_____ declare   C. a loyalty, a commitment to something

_____ allegiance   D. a dense group of shrubs, bushes or small trees

Day 90
Continued

Circle one option from each set of choices. It's best to choose different options for each dog. After you make your choices, you can draw a picture of each if you like.

MOM DOG:
Hair: long or short
Body: big or small or medium
Legs: long or short
Ears: long or short
Coat: solid or spotted
Color: brown or white or black
Tail: long or short

DAD DOG:
Hair: long or short
Body: big or small or medium
Legs: long or short
Ears: long or short
Coat: solid or spotted
Color: brown or white or black
Tail: long or short

For each trait, circle either odd or even.

Hair: odd/even   Ears: odd/even   Body: odd/even   Tail: odd/even
Legs: odd/even   Coat: odd/even   Color: odd/even

Now, build your baby dog. Ask your parent to read you the rest of the instructions.

Hair: long or short
Body: big or small or medium
Legs: long or short
Ears: long or short
Coat: solid or spotted
Color: brown or white or black
Tail: long or short

Day 91

Spelling Words

_____   _____

_____   _____

Underline the nouns that are people, places, or things.

1. Sarah asked to go to the beach for her

    birthday.

2. My mom and dad went on a picnic at the

    park.

3. The boy in the red shirt played with his

    small, hairy dog.

4. The mailman dropped off a package in front

    of our door.

Day 92

Spelling Words

_____   _____

_____   _____

Write in a noun that completes the compound word. There can be more than one answer.

snow_____

cup_____

cow_____

base_____

play_____

Day 93

Spelling Words

_____   _____

_____   _____

Circle the animals that live in the grasslands.

Day 94

Spelling Words

_____   _____

_____   _____

Design the money for your kingdom. What is it called? How much is it worth? In other words, how much does it cost to buy say, a dollar-store toy in your money?

_____

Day 95

Spelling Words

_____   _____

_____   _____

_____   _____

_____   _____

_____   _____

_____   _____

_____   _____

Write in the letter of the definition for each word.

_____ purchase   A. accepted as normal, or a level of quality

_____ standard   B. something you have

_____ refuse   C. to buy

_____ possession   D. to say no to doing something, or to refuse to
                            give permission to do something

Day 96

Write a sentence using one of the vocabulary words. Draw a picture that illustrates the meaning of the other. inhabitant – pillar

_____

_____

Draw a picture of a wheel and axel or of a wedge at work.

Day 97

Write a sentence using one of the vocabulary words. Draw a picture that illustrates the meaning of the other. furnace – settle

_____

_____

Write the plurals by following the rules. Take off the end of the word to change the F into VES. If it ends in a CH, add ES. Otherwise, add S.

Example:

wife   wives

leaf   _____

peach   _____

toy   _____

yourself   _____

Day 98

Write a sentence using one of the vocabulary words. Draw a picture that illustrates the meaning of the other. integrity – restore

_____

_____

Write a question. Make sure it begins with a capital letter and ends with a question mark.

_____

_____

Write the answer. Make sure it starts with a capital letter and ends with a period or exclamation point.

_____

_____

Day 99

Write a sentence using one of the vocabulary words. Draw a picture that illustrates the meaning of the other. wean – distress

_____

_____

Add a double letter and then the ending. Read the word!

Example:

hop   -ing   hopping

hug   -ed   _____

sip   -ing   _____

tag   -ing   _____

drop   -ed   _____

Day 100

Write a sentence using one of the vocabulary words. Draw a picture that illustrates the meaning of the other. redeem – seize

_____

_____

Write a knock knock joke. Here's an example. Make sure you use the correct punctuation.

Knock, knock.
Who's there?
Lettuce.
Lettuce who?
Lettuce in! It's cold out here!

_____

_____

_____

_____

_____

Day 101

Write a sentence using one of the vocabulary words. Draw a picture that illustrates the meaning of the other. offering – journey

_____

_____

Draw a picture showing how a water wheel works. Water runs into the wheel, fills the buckets/shelves with water, which weighs it down so that it turns.

Day 102

Write a sentence using one of the vocabulary words. Draw a picture that illustrates the meaning of the other. bound – thicket

_____

_____

Draw pictures or act to show the words as nouns and as verbs.

	NOUN	**VERB**
SAND or DIE		
PLAY		

Day 103

Write a sentence using one of the vocabulary words. Draw a picture that illustrates the meaning of the other. declare – allegiance

_____

_____

A pronoun replaces a noun. Write a pronoun to replace the nouns given.

Example:

your name   I

you and your family   _____

Sarah   _____

James and John   _____

cup   _____

Day 104

Write a sentence using one of the vocabulary words. Draw a picture that illustrates the meaning of the other. refuse – standard

_____

_____

You are going to write the past tense of the verbs. Think: Today I ____. Yesterday I _____.

Example:

run   ran

talk   _____

give   _____

tell   _____

Day 105

Write a sentence using one of the vocabulary words. Draw a picture that illustrates the meaning of the other. possession – purchase

_____

_____

Write the two words as a contraction or the contraction as two words.

Example:

hadn't   had not

can't   _____

it is   _____

would not   _____

isn't   _____

Day 106 Spelling Words

_____   _____

_____   _____

Day 107 Spelling Words

_____   _____

_____   _____

Day 108 Spelling Words

_____   _____

_____   _____

Day 109 Spelling Words

_____   _____

_____   _____

Day 110 Spelling Words

_____   _____

_____   _____

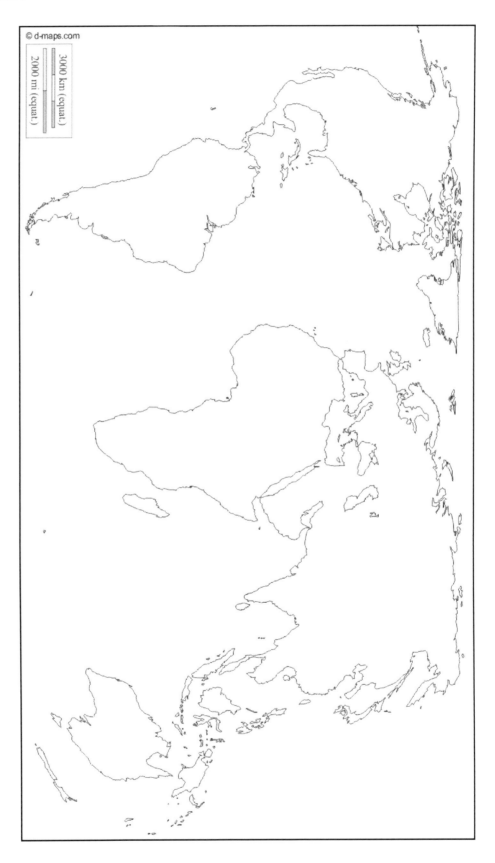

Day 107

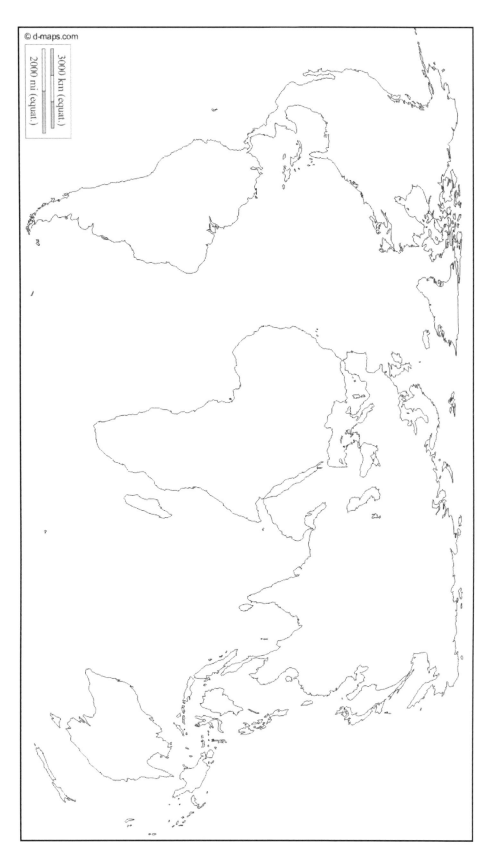

Day 108

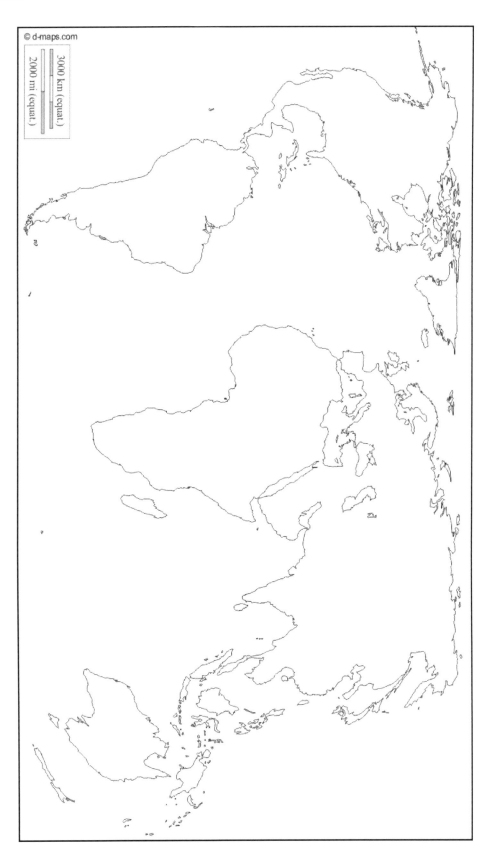

Day 109

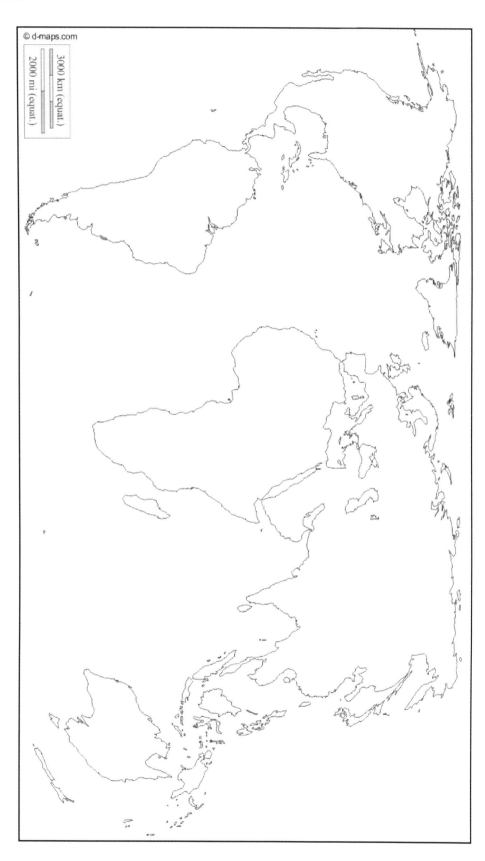

Day 110

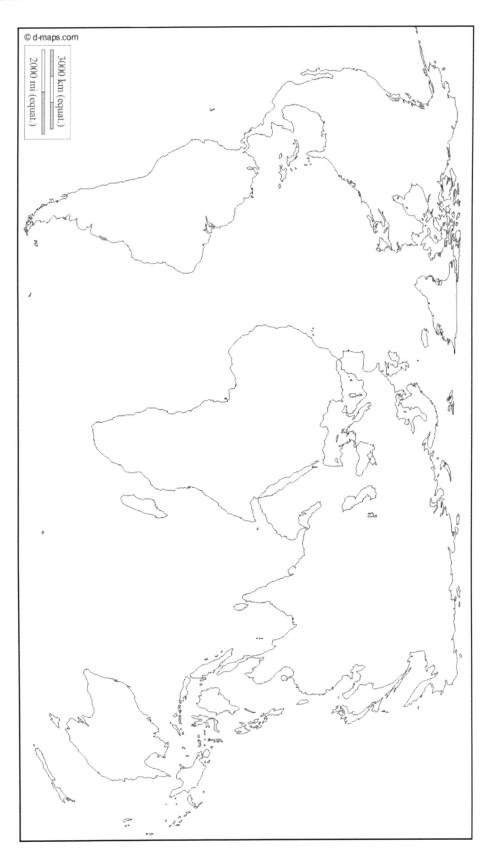

Day 111

Spelling Words

_____   _____

_____   _____

Match the terms to the
skeleton.

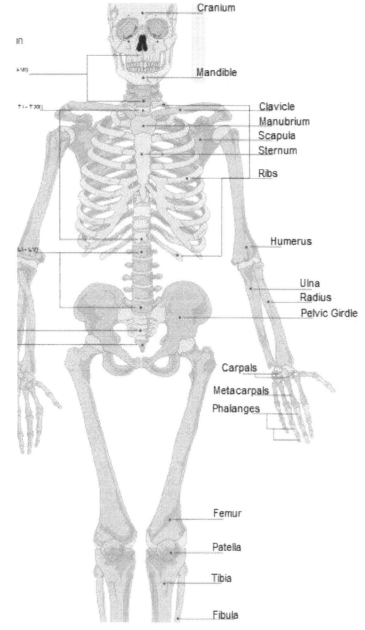

clavicle

cranium

patella

mandible

Can you find other
phalanges?

Day 112

Spelling Words

_____   _____

_____   _____

Here are some pictures of troughs. What are the animals doing? Think of ways the animals could use the troughs.

Day 113

Spelling Words

_____   _____

_____   _____

Make a family tree for Rebekah and Isaac.

Day 114

Spelling Words

_____   _____

_____   _____

Write a simple sentence. Then rewrite it adding as many adjectives as you can before the noun to describe it. For example: I like dogs. I like cute, cuddly, furry, drooly, hairy, excited, friendly dogs. You could draw a picture of what you described.

_____

_____

_____

_____

Day 115

Spelling Words

_____   _____

_____   _____

_____   _____

_____   _____

_____   _____

_____   _____

_____   _____

Write in the letter of the definition for each word.

_____ oath   A. worth a lot

_____ trough   B. getting, accomplishing what you wanted

_____ valuable   C. a long container open on top, used for animals to drink

_____ successful   D. promises that must be kept as if something bad might

Day 116

Spelling Words

_____   _____

_____   _____

Write a sentence that's a question. Then write the answer.

_____

_____

_____

Color in Joseph's tunic.

Day 117

Spelling Words

_____   _____

_____   _____

Write the possessive by adding an apostrophe S.

Example:

father, flock   father's flock

Olive, books   _____

dog, collar   _____

cat, toys   _____

house, address   _____

sky, color   _____

Day 118

Spelling Words

_____   _____

_____   _____

Write the plurals by following the rules. Normally, you just add an S. Words that end in CH, SH, S, or X get an ES added on to make them plural.

Example:

branch   branches

wish   _____

kiss   _____

box   _____

friend   _____

lunch   _____

Day 119

Spelling Words

_____   _____

_____   _____

Add ING onto the end of the words. Do you remember adding a double letter? Hop became hopping with two P's. We did that so that it didn't read hope-ing. To write hope-ing we drop the E. If the vowel already says its name without a silent E, you can just add ING.

Example:

hope   hoping
hop   hopping

tape   _____

tap   _____

game   _____

can   _____

read   _____

Day 120

Spelling Words

_____   _____

_____   _____

_____   _____

_____   _____

_____   _____

_____   _____

_____   _____

Write in the letter of the definition for each word.

_____ rebuke   A. to scold

_____ graze   B. to get a benefit, often refers to money

_____ balm   C. anything that heals or soothes

_____ profit   D. to eat grass or crops in a field, to eat little by
                          little throughout the day

Day 121

Spelling Words

_____   _____

_____   _____

Write in a noun that completes the compound word. There can be more than one answer.

some_____

my_____

with_____

Write a sentence that includes a compound word.

_____

_____

_____

Day 122

Spelling Words

_____   _____

_____   _____

Write the past tense of these verbs.

play   _____

talk   _____

Write a sentence with the past tense.

_____

_____

_____

Day 123

Spelling Words

_____   _____

_____   _____

Write your name, add an apostrophe S, and write what belongs to you.

_____

Write a sentence that includes a possessive. Write about something that belongs to you.

_____

_____

_____

Day 124

Spelling Words

_____   _____

_____   _____

Draw a picture that demonstrates one of your rights!

Day 125

Spelling Words

_____   _____

_____   _____

_____   _____

_____   _____

_____   _____

_____   _____

_____   _____

Write in the letter of the definition for each word.

_____ prosper   A. really angry

_____ garment   B. a piece of clothing

_____ supervise   C. to succeed financially or physically

_____ furious   D. to keep watch over someone while they work

Day 126

Spelling Words

_____   _____

_____   _____

Write molecule names. You could draw them too if you like. H_2O is a water molecule. It has two hydrogen atoms and one oxygen atom. You could draw it like this H-O-H or draw circles for the atoms. Lines connect the atoms into a single molecule.

Write $NaHCO_3$.
sodium hydrogen carbonate

Hydrogen Chloride, HCl
Carbon Dioxide, CO_2
Sulfur Dioxide, SO_2
Hydrogen Peroxide, HOOH

Day 127

Spelling Words

_____   _____

_____   _____

Write two sentences. Circle the subject noun and the verb that goes with it in each sentence.

_____

_____

_____

_____

_____

Day 128

Spelling Words

_____   _____

_____   _____

Write your name, add an apostrophe S, and write what belongs to you.

_____

Draw a picture of a healthy plant getting everything it needs.

Day 129

Spelling Words

_____   _____

_____   _____

Write two sentences. Circle the subject noun and the verb that goes with it in each sentence.

_____

_____

_____

_____

_____

Day 130

Spelling Words

_____   _____

_____   _____

_____   _____

_____   _____

_____   _____

_____   _____

_____   _____

Write in the letter of the definition for each word.

_____ interpretation   A. the explanation of something's meaning

_____ gaunt   B. a lot of something

_____ appoint   C. especially looking thin from hunger

_____ abundance   D. to set someone in charge over something

Day 131

Write a sentence using one of the vocabulary words. Draw a picture that illustrates the meaning of the other. complete – weep

_____

_____

Draw a picture of a wheel and axle at work.

Day 132

Write a sentence using one of the vocabulary words. Draw a picture that illustrates the meaning of the other. fortunate – sorrow

_____

_____

Write the plurals by following the rules. Normally, you just add an S. Words that end in CH, SH, S, or X get an ES added on to make them plural.

Example:

beach   beaches

lunch   _____

push   _____

mess   _____

friend   _____

Day 133

Write a sentence using one of the vocabulary words. Draw a picture that illustrates the meaning of the other. trough – swear

_____

_____

Write a question. Make sure it begins with a capital letter and ends with a question mark.

_____

_____

Write the answer. Make sure it starts with a capital letter and ends with a period or exclamation point.

_____

_____

Day 134

Write a sentence using one of the vocabulary words. Draw a picture that illustrates the meaning of the other. successful – valuable

_____

_____

Add ING onto the end of the words. To write hope-ing we drop the E. If the vowel already says its name without a silent E, you can just add ING.

Example:

hope   hoping
hop   hopping

name   _____

tip   _____

frame   _____

fan   _____

Day 135

Write a sentence using one of the vocabulary words. Draw a picture that illustrates the meaning of the other. graze – rebuke

_____

_____

Find continents.

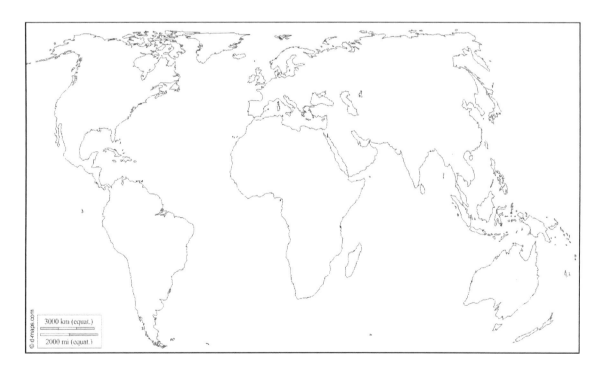

North America, South America, Asia, Africa, Europe, Australia

Day 136

Write a sentence using one of the vocabulary words. Draw a picture that illustrates the meaning of the other. appoint – abundance

_____

_____

Write adjectives. Describe the noun.

Example:

kid   tall

building   _____

yard   _____

book   _____

Day 137

Write a sentence using one of the vocabulary words. Draw a picture that illustrates the meaning of the other. balm – profit

_____

_____

Write the possessive by adding an apostrophe S.

Example:

father, flock   father's flock

boy, book   _____

dog, leash   _____

cat, yarn   _____

house, yard   _____

Day 138

Write a sentence using one of the vocabulary words. Draw a picture that illustrates the meaning of the other. prosper – garment

_____

_____

Draw a picture of a camel, lion, or cow and tell what you know about them.

Day 139

Write a sentence using one of the vocabulary words. Draw a picture that illustrates the meaning of the other. furious – supervise

_____

_____

Write the past tense of these verbs.

name _____

step _____
(needs a double letter)

Write a sentence with the past tense.

_____

_____

Day 140

Write a sentence using one of the vocabulary words. Draw a picture that illustrates the meaning of the other. interpretation – gaunt

_____

_____

Draw a healthy plant and a patella.

Day 141

Spelling Plan

☐ I want to work on spelling.

☐ I will correct my spelling when I write.

☐ I will make spelling crafts.

☐ I will play Spelling Bees.

☐ I will _____.

☐ I will do spelling every day.

☐ I will do spelling once a week.

☐ I will do spelling every day for one week.

☐ I will do spelling _____.

☐ I will use my GC spelling lists.

☐ I will use words I have misspelled in the past.

☐ I will use one spelling word at a time.

☐ I will use one spelling list at a time.

☐ _____

☐ _____

☐ Days 146 -1 50   ☐ Days 151 – 155   ☐ Days 156 – 160

☐ Days 161 – 165   ☐ Days 166 – 170   ☐ Days 171 - 180

Day 142

Vocabulary Plan

☐ I want to work on vocabulary.

☐ I will use my vocabulary words when I write.

☐ I will play Pictionary.

☐ I will play charades.

☐ I will _____.

☐ I will do vocabulary every day.

☐ I will do vocabulary once a week. _____

☐ I will do vocabulary every day for one week. _____

☐ I will do vocabulary _____.

☐ I will use my GC vocabulary lists.

☐ I will only use words I have trouble remembering.

☐ I will use one vocabulary word at a time.

☐ I will use one vocabulary list at a time.

☐ _____

☐ _____

☐ Days 146 -1 50   ☐ Days 151 – 155   ☐ Days 156 – 160

☐ Days 161 – 165   ☐ Days 166 – 170   ☐ Days 171 - 180

Day 143

Writing Plan

☐ I want to work on writing.

☐ I will write words.

☐ I will write sentences.

☐ I will write stories.

☐ I will write letters.

☐ I will _____.

☐ I will do writing every day.

☐ I will do writing once a week. _____

☐ I will do writing every day for one week. _____

☐ I will do writing _____.

☐ _____

☐ _____

☐ Days 146 -1 50   ☐ Days 151 – 155   ☐ Days 156 – 160

☐ Days 161 – 165   ☐ Days 166 – 170   ☐ Days 171 - 180

Day 144

Science Plan

☐ I want to work on science.

☐ I will do experiments.

☐ I will read books.

☐ I will watch videos.

☐ I will _____.

☐ I will do science every day.

☐ I will do science once a week. _____

☐ I will do science every day for one week. _____

☐ I will do science _____.

☐ I will use my GC lesson list.

☐ I will use science topics I want to learn more about.

☐ I will make a project.

☐ I will tell others what I have learned.

☐ _____

☐ _____

☐ Days 146 -1 50   ☐ Days 151 – 155   ☐ Days 156 – 160

☐ Days 161 – 165   ☐ Days 166 – 170   ☐ Days 171 - 180

Day 145

Social Studies Plan

☐ I want to work on social studies.

☐ I will read books.

☐ I will watch videos.

☐ I will _____.

☐ I will do social studies every day.

☐ I will do social studies once a week. _____

☐ I will do social studies every day for one week. _____

☐ I will do social studies _____.

☐ I will use my GC lesson list.

☐ I will use social studies topics I want to learn more about.

☐ I will put on a play.

☐ I will tell others what I have learned.

☐ _____

☐ _____

☐ Days 146 -1 50   ☐ Days 151 – 155   ☐ Days 156 – 160

☐ Days 161 – 165   ☐ Days 166 – 170   ☐ Days 171 - 180

The Periodic Table of Elements

1 hydrogen H 1.0079																	2 helium He 4.0026
3 lithium Li 6.941	4 beryllium Be 9.0122											5 boron B 10.811	6 carbon C 12.011	7 nitrogen N 14.007	8 oxygen O 15.999	9 fluorine F 18.998	10 neon Ne 20.180
11 sodium Na 22.990	12 magnesium Mg 24.305											13 aluminium Al 26.962	14 silicon Si 28.086	15 phosphorus P 30.974	16 sulfur S 32.065	17 chlorine Cl 35.453	18 argon Ar 39.948
19 potassium K 39.098	20 calcium Ca 40.078	21 scandium Sc 44.956	22 titanium Ti 47.867	23 vanadium V 50.942	24 chromium Cr 51.996	25 manganese Mn 54.938	26 iron Fe 55.845	27 cobalt Co 58.933	28 nickel Ni 58.693	29 copper Cu 63.546	30 zinc Zn 65.39	31 gallium Ga 69.723	32 germanium Ge 72.61	33 arsenic As 74.922	34 selenium Se 78.96	35 bromine Br 79.904	36 krypton Kr 83.80
37 rubidium Rb 85.468	38 strontium Sr 87.62	39 yttrium Y 88.906	40 zirconium Zr 91.224	41 niobium Nb 92.906	42 molybdenum Mo 95.94	43 technetium Tc [98]	44 ruthenium Ru 101.07	45 rhodium Rh 102.91	46 palladium Pd 106.42	47 silver Ag 107.87	48 cadmium Cd 112.41	49 indium In 114.82	50 tin Sn 118.71	51 antimony Sb 121.76	52 tellurium Te 127.60	53 iodine I 126.90	54 xenon Xe 131.29
55 caesium Cs 132.91	56 barium Ba 137.33	57-70 *	71 lutetium Lu 174.97	72 hafnium Hf 178.49	73 tantalum Ta 180.95	74 tungsten W 183.84	75 rhenium Re 186.21	76 osmium Os 190.23	77 iridium Ir 192.22	78 platinum Pt 195.08	79 gold Au 196.97	80 mercury Hg 200.59	81 thallium Tl 204.38	82 lead Pb 207.2	83 bismuth Bi 208.98	84 polonium Po [209]	85 astatine At [210]	86 radon Rn [222]
87 francium Fr [223]	88 radium Ra [226]	89-102 **	103 lawrencium Lr [262]	104 rutherfordium Rf [261]	105 dubnium Db [262]	106 seaborgium Sg [266]	107 bohrium Bh [264]	108 hassium Hs [269]	109 meitnerium Mt [268]	110 ununnilium Uun [271]	111 unununium Uuu [272]	112 ununbium Uub [277]		114 ununquadium Uuq [289]				

* Lanthanide series

57 lanthanum La 138.91	58 cerium Ce 140.12	59 praseodymium Pr 140.91	60 neodymium Nd 144.24	61 promethium Pm [145]	62 samarium Sm 150.36	63 europium Eu 151.96	64 gadolinium Gd 157.25	65 terbium Tb 158.93	66 dysprosium Dy 162.50	67 holmium Ho 164.93	68 erbium Er 167.26	69 thulium Tm 168.93	70 ytterbium Yb 173.04

** Actinide series

89 actinium Ac [227]	90 thorium Th 232.04	91 protactinium Pa 231.04	92 uranium U 238.03	93 neptunium Np [237]	94 plutonium Pu [244]	95 americium Am [243]	96 curium Cm [247]	97 berkelium Bk [247]	98 californium Cf [251]	99 einsteinium Es [252]	100 fermium Fm [257]	101 mendelevium Md [258]	102 nobelium No [259]

Thank you for using
Genesis Curriculum
The Book of Genesis

We hope you had a great year learning together.

Genesis Curriculum also offers:

GC Steps: This is GC's preschool and kindergarten curriculum. There are three years (ages three through six) where kids will learn to read and write as well as develop beginning math skills.

A Mind for Math: This is GC's elementary school learning-together math program based on the curriculum's daily Bible reading. Children work together as well as have their own leveled workbook.

Rainbow Readers: These are leveled reading books. They each have a unique dictionary with the included words underlined in the text. They are also updated to use modern American spelling.

Look for more years of the Genesis Curriculum using both Old and New Testament books of the Bible. Find us online to read about the latest developments in this expanding curriculum.

GenesisCurriculum.com

Made in the USA
Coppell, TX
25 August 2020